Liquid Love

Quotes For The Love Of Water

Leslie Gabriel

ISBN 978-1-7350563-1-9

https://www.watercelebration.org/

Table of Contents

Forward...4

Water in Politics 6

Water in Spirituality 17

Water in Humor..28

Water in the Environment 39

Water in Love 50

Water in Science...61

Water in Money..72

Water in Wisdom 83

Acknowledgments 96

About the Author 98

H2O Activists References 100

Photographic References 106

Forward

As I grow through life, I have started to realize what has made the biggest difference for me. When I honor the source of my existence, I notice that find the most satisfaction.

All of us are closely related to water. But, we may have forgotten the ties that bind.

We all start in water – in our mommy's belly – resting, breathing, feeding and growing in water.

Of course we all need water to live – that is a no brainer. Of course, water is directly linked to our survival as a species and to the survival of our blue planet. Of course, both our earth and humanity is comprised of about 75% water. But, there is more.

Water also has direct connections to the entire culture. H_2O is closely connected to music, art, science, love, spirituality, philosophy, religion, medicine and economics. Plus, water references have been abundantly sprinkled through our human language.

Water in our language you ask? I declare a resounding YES!

Water in language can represent "all of it". It's the big picture, the big metaphor, the big idea. Simultaneously, water in language can represent the smallest common denominator. It is the parable that all of us can understand. Sometimes the water reference is merely mundane, like a stagnant pool of mucky H_2O.

All the while, human language, the building block of our shared reality has a steady stream of references to water.

Just think of a few you have used …
- "Go with the flow."
- "What a drip!"
- "I hate to rain on your parade, but … "

Think of a few more. Start to become aware of where you reference is in your language.

It is my request that you use this book to begin a journey to the center of water ... a journey you will never regret. On this journey, you will get related to the source of all life, in a new and perhaps profound way.

Then, look at your own life and see where your relationship to H2O resides.

I assert that water language is a solution to have us all get reconnected with everything in life ... even life itself.

Let this book move through you like a gently running brook. Let it splash upon the shores of your consciousness. Let it show you a way to wade back into the interconnectedness of your daily life.

Allow yourself to be inspired by the moistness of it all. Start to see water outside of the cup. Let yourself see a different side of H2O.

Through this new view – this new transformed view – look at other areas of your life that you may have taken for granted ... like water.

Notice the value. Respect the source. Revere your own life. For only with love and reverence will we care for all that matters most.

Let it show you a way to find your own stream, wherever that may be and to wherever the river may lead.

Yours Truly For The Love Of Water,

Leslie Gabriel
Ambassador For Water

Water in Politics

"No, no, we are not satisfied, and we will not be satisfied until justice rolls down like waters and righteousness like a mighty stream."

- Martin Luther King, Jr.

Martin Luther King, Jr. (January 15, 1929 – April 4, 1968), was an American clergyman, activist and prominent leader in the African-American civil rights movement. His main legacy was to secure progress on civil rights in the United States and he is frequently referenced as a human rights icon today.

"Water, like religion and ideology, has the power to move millions of people. Since the very birth of human civilization, people have moved to settle close to it. People move when there is too little of it. People move when there is too much of it. People journey down it. People write, sing and dance about it. People fight over it. And all people, everywhere and every day, need it."

-Mikhail Gorbachev

Mikhail Sergeyevich Gorbachev (Born 2 March 1931) was the last General Secretary of the Communist Party of the Soviet Union, serving from 1985 until 1991, and also the last head of state of the USSR, serving from 1988 until its collapse in 1991. He was the only Soviet leader to have been born after the October Revolution of 1917.

"Anyone who can solve the problems of water will be worthy of two Nobel prizes - one for peace and one for science."

- John F. Kennedy

John Fitzgerald "Jack" Kennedy (May 29, 1917 – November 22, 1963), often referred to by his initials JFK, was the 35th President of the United States, serving from 1961 until his assassination in 1963.

"When the water starts boiling it is foolish to turn off the heat."

- Nelson Mandela

Nelson Rolihlahla Mandela; born 18 July 1918 in Transkei, South Africa is a former President of South Africa, the first to be elected in a fully representative democratic election, who held office from 1994–99. Before his presidency, Mandela was an anti-apartheid activist, and the leader of the African National Congress's armed wing Umkhonto we Sizwe.

"No one has the right to use America's rivers and America's Waterways, that belong to all the people, as a sewer. The banks of a river may belong to one man or one industry or one State, but the waters which flow between the banks should belong to all the people."

- Lyndon B. Johnson

Lyndon Baines Johnson (August 27, 1908 – January 22, 1973), often referred to as LBJ, served as the 36th President of the United States from 1963 to 1969 after his service as the Vice President of the United States from 1961 to 1963.

"Water is the most precious, limited natural resource we have in this country...But because water belongs to no one - except the people - special interests, including government polluters, use it as their private sewers."

- Ralph Nader

Ralph Nader (born February 27, 1934) is an American attorney, author, lecturer, political activist, and candidate for President of the United States as an independent candidate in 2004 and 2008, and a Green Party candidate in 1996 and 2000.

"If there is no struggle, there is no progress.
Those who profess to favor freedom, and
deprecate agitation, are men who want crops
without plowing up the ground, they want rain
without thunder and lightning."

- Frederick Douglass

Frederick Douglass (born Frederick Augustus Washington Bailey, (born circa 1818 – February 20, 1895) was an American abolitionist, women's suffragist, editor, orator, author, statesman and reformer.

"The tree of liberty grows only when watered by the blood of tyrants."

- Bertrand Barere de Vieuzac

Bertrand Barère de Vieuzac (September 10, 1755 – January 13, 1841) was a French politician and journalist, one of the most notorious members of the National Convention during the French Revolution.

"A sincere diplomat is like dry water
or wooden iron."

- Joseph Stalin

oseph Vissarionovich Stalin (born Ioseb Besarionis dze Jughashvili in
Georgian or Iosif Vissarionovich Dzhugashvili in Russian patronymic no-
menclature; 18 December 1878 – 5 March 1953) was the first General Secre-
ary of the Communist Party of the Soviet Union's Central Committee from
1922 until his death in 1953.

"On matters of style, swim with the current, on matters of principle, stand like a rock."

- Thomas Jefferson

Thomas Jefferson (April 13, 1743 – July 4, 1826) was the third President of the United States (1801–1809), the principal author of the Declaration of Independence (1776), and—for his promotion of the ideals of republicanism in the United States—one of the most influential Founding Fathers.

Water in Spirituality

"Before enlightenment, Chop wood, Carry water.
After enlightenment, Chop wood, Carry water."

- Zen saying

Zen is a school of Mahāyāna Buddhism, translated from the Chinese word Chán. Chán is itself derived from the Sanskrit Dhyāna, which means "meditation".

Zen emphasizes experiential Prajñā—particularly as realized in the form of meditation known as zazen—in the attainment of awakening, often simply called the path of enlightenment.

"Water sustains all."

- Thales of Miletus, 600 B.C.

Thales of Miletus, (ca. 624 BC–ca. 546 BC), was a pre-Socratic Greek philosopher from Miletus in Asia Minor, and one of the Seven Sages of Greece. Many, most notably Aristotle, regard him as the first philosopher in the Greek tradition. According to Bertrand Russell, "Western philosophy begins with Thales."

"Let yourself be open and life will be easier. A spoon of salt in a glass of water makes the water undrinkable. A spoon of salt in a lake is almost unnoticed."

- Hindu Prince Gautama Siddhartha, Buddha

Siddhārtha Gautama was a spiritual teacher in the north eastern region of the Indian subcontinent who founded Buddhism. He is generally seen by Buddhists as the Supreme Buddha (Sammāsambuddha) of our age. The time of his birth and death are uncertain.

"By means of water, we give life to everything."

- Qur'an, 21:30

The Qur'an (literally "the recitation"; also sometimes transliterated as Qu-an, Qur'ān, Koran, Alcoran or Al-Qur'ān) is the central religious text of Islam. Muslims believe the Qur'an to be the book of divine guidance and direction for mankind, and consider the original Arabic text to be the final revelation of God.

"Living creatures are nourished by food, and food is nourished by rain; rain itself is the water of life, which comes from selfless worship and service."

- The Bhagavad Gita

The Bhagavad Gita (Bhagavad Gītā, "Song of God") is one of the most important Hindu scriptures. It is revered as a sacred scripture of Hinduism, and considered as one of the most important philosophical classics of the world. The Bhagavad Gita comprising 700 verses, is a part of the Mahabharata.

"We call upon the waters that rim the earth, horizon to horizon, that flow in our rivers and streams, that fall upon our gardens and fields, and we ask that they teach us and show us the way."

- Chinook Indian Blessing

Chinook Indian refers to several groups of Native Americans in the Pacific Northwest region of the United States. In the early 19th century, the Chinookan peoples lived along the lower and middle Columbia River in present-day Oregon and Washington. The Chinookan tribes were those encountered by the Lewis and Clark Expedition in 1805 on the lower Columbia.

"Water is also one of the four elements, the most beautiful of God's creations.

It is both wet and cold, heavy, and with a tendency to descend, and flows with great readiness.

It is this the Holy Scripture has in view when it says, And the darkness was upon the face of the deep. And the Spirit of God moved upon the face of the waters.

Water, then, is the most beautiful element and rich in usefulness, and purifies from all filth, and not only from the filth of the body but from that of the soul, if it should have received the grace of the Spirit. "

- St. John of Damascus

Saint John of Damascus (c. 676 – 4 December 749) was a monk and priest from Damascus. He was born and raised in that city, and died at his monastery Mar Saba.

"The trees reflected in the river, they are
unconscious of a spiritual world so
near to them. So are we."

- Nathaniel Hawthorne

Nathaniel Hawthorne (born Nathaniel Hathorne; July 4, 1804 – May 19, 1864) was an American novelist and short story writer.

"Be praised, My Lord, through Sister Water; she is very useful, and humble, and precious, and pure."

- St. Francis of Assisi

Saint Francis of Assisi (Giovanni Francesco Bernardone; born 1181/1182 – October 3, 1226) was a Catholic deacon and the founder of the Order of Friars Minor, more commonly known as the Franciscans. He is known as the patron saint of animals, the environment and Italy.

"We can't help being thirsty, moving toward the voice of water.

Milk drinkers draw close to the mother.

Muslims, Christians, Jews, Buddhists, Hindus, Shamans, everyone hears the intelligent sound and moves with thirst to meet it."

- Rumi

Mawlānā Jalāl ad-Dīn Muḥammad Balkhī, also known as Jalāl ad-Dīn Muḥammad Rūmī, but known to the English-speaking world simply as Rumi, (30 September 1207 – 17 December 1273), was a 13th-century Persian poet, Islamic jurist, theologian, and mystic.

Water in Humor

"You can't trust water. Even a straight stick turns crooked in it."

- W.C. Fields

William Claude Dukenfield (January 29, 1880 – December 25, 1946), better known as W. C. Fields, was an American comedian, actor, juggler and writer. Fields created one of the great American comic personas of the first half of the 20th century.

"If you're not part of the solution, you're part of the precipitate."

- Steven Wright

Steven Alexander Wright (born December 6, 1955) is an American comedian, actor and writer. He is known for his distinctly lethargic voice and slow, deadpan delivery of ironic, witty, philosophical and sometimes deeply confusing or nonsensical jokes and one-liners with contrived situations.

"My wife's a water sign. I'm an earth sign. Together we make mud."

- Rodney Dangerfield

Rodney Dangerfield (November 22, 1921 – October 5, 2004), born Jacob Cohen, was an American comedian and actor, best known for the catch-phrases "I don't get no respect" or "I get no respect" and his monologues on that theme.

"Basically my wife was immature. I'd be at home in the bath and she'd come in and sink my boats."

- Woody Allen

Woody Allen (born Allen Stewart Konigsberg; December 1, 1935) is an American screenwriter, film director, actor, comedian, writer, musician, and playwright.

"Aquafina ... I think it means the end of water as we know it."

- Lewis Black

Lewis Niles Black (born August 30, 1948) is an American stand-up comedian, author, playwright and actor. He is known for his comedy style which often includes simulating a mental breakdown or an increasingly angry rant, ridiculing history, politics, religion, trends and cultural phenomena.

"Ever wonder about those people who spend $2 apiece on those little bottles of Evian water? Try spelling Evian backward."

- George Carlin

George Denis Patrick Carlin (May 12, 1937 – June 22, 2008) was an American stand-up comedian, social critic, actor, and author, who won five Grammy Awards for his comedy albums. Carlin was noted for his black humor as well as his thoughts on politics, the English language, psychology, religion, and various taboo subjects.

"You'll notice that Bush never speaks when Cheney is drinking water, check that shit out."

- Robin Williams

Robin McLaurim Williams (July 21, 1951 - August 11, 2014) is an American actor and comedian. Rising to fame with his role as the alien Mork in the TV series Mork and Mindy, and later stand up comedy work, Williams has performed in many feature films since 1980. He won the Academy Award for Best Supporting Actor for his performance in the 1997 film Good Will Hunting.

"The formula for water is H_2O. Is the formula for an ice cube H_2O squared?"

- Lily Tomlin

Mary Jean "Lily" Tomlin (born September 1, 1939) is an American actress, comedian, writer and producer. She has won multiple awards from many quarters, including Tony Awards, Emmy Awards, and a Grammy Award and has also been nominated for an Academy Award.

"Let me tell me you of a bygone age of fairies and trolls, when I was your age water came out of a magic faucet. "

- Brad Stine

Brad Stine (born 1960) is an American stand-up comedian, actor, and author. Relatively unknown until 2003, Stine first gained exposure when he "came out" as a conservative Christian on his debut album, Put a Helmet On!

"If your body is 90 percent water, why have you
got to drink water all the time? Why can't
you just have some crisps?"

- Russell Brand

Russell Brand (born 4 June 1975) is an English comedian, actor, radio host, author, and activist. After beginning his career as a stand-up comedian, Brand first achieved renown in 2004 as the host of Big Brother's Big Mouth, a Big Brother spin-off. Over the course of his career, Brand has been the subject of frequent media coverage and controversy for his controversial public antics.

Water in the Environment

"We forget that the water cycle and the
life cycle are one. "

- Jacques Cousteau

Jacques-Yves Cousteau (11 June 1910 – 25 June 1997) was a French naval
officer, explorer, ecologist, filmmaker, innovator, scientist, photographer,
author and researcher who studied the sea and all forms of life in water.

"To find the universal elements enough; to find the air and the water exhilarating; to be refreshed by a morning walk or an evening saunter; to be thrilled by the stars at night; to be elated over a bird's nest or a wildflower in spring - these are some of the rewards of the simple life."

- John Burroughs

John Burroughs (April 3, 1837 – March 29, 1921) was an American naturalist and nature essayist important in the evolution of the U.S. conservation movement.

"Have you also learned that secret from the river; that there is no such thing as time? That the river is everywhere at the same time, at the source and at the mouth, at the waterfall, at the ferry, at the current, in the ocean and in the mountains, everywhere and that the present only exists for it, not the shadow of the past nor the shadow of the future."

- Hermann Hesse

Hermann Karl Hesse (2 July, 1877 – 9 August, 1962) was a German-born Swiss poet, novelist, and painter. His best-known works include Demian, Steppenwolf, Siddhartha, and The Glass Bead Game, each of which explores an individual's search for authenticity, self-knowledge and spirituality. In 1946, he received the Nobel Prize in Literature.

"The world is mud-luscious and puddle-wonderful. "

- E.E. Cummings

Edward Estlin Cummings (October 14, 1894 – September 3, 1962), popularly known as E. E. Cummings, with the abbreviated form of his name often written by others in lowercase letters as e. e. cummings (in the style of some of his poems), was an American poet, painter, essayist, author, and playwright.

"To stand at the edge of the sea, to sense the ebb and flow of the tides, to feelthe breath of a mist moving over a great salt marsh, to watch the flight of shore birds that have swept up and down the surf lines of the continents for untold thousands of year, to see the running of the old eels and the young shad to the sea, is to have knowledge of things that are as nearly eternal as any earthly life can be."

- Rachel Carson

Rachel Louise Carson (May 27, 1907 – April 14, 1964) was an American marine biologist and nature writer whose writings are credited with advancing the global environmental movement.

"Nature chose for a tool, not the earthquake or lightning to rend and split asunder, not the stormy torrent or eroding rain, but the tender snow-flowers noiselessly falling through unnumbered centuries."

- John Muir

ohn Muir (21 April 1838 – 24 December 1914) was a Scottish-born American naturalist, author, and early advocate of preservation of wilderness in he United States. His letters, essays, and books telling of his adventures in nature, especially in the Sierra Nevada mountains of California, have been ead by millions.

"A lake is the landscape's most beautiful and expressive feature. It is earth's eye; looking into which the beholder measures the depth of his own nature."

- Henry David Thoreau

Henry David Thoreau (born David Henry Thoreau; July 12, 1817 – May 6 1862) was an American author, poet, naturalist, tax resister, developmen critic, surveyor, historian, philosopher, and leading transcendentalist.

"Every human should have the idea of taking care of the environment, of nature, of water. So using too much or wasting water should have some kind of feeling or sense of concern. Some sort of responsibility and with that, a sense of discipline."

- The 14th Dalai Lama Tenzin Gyatso

Jetsun Jamphel Ngawang Lobsang Yeshe Tenzin Gyatso (born Lhamo Dön-drub) is the 14th Dalai Lama, a spiritual leader revered among the people of Tibet. He is the head of the government-in-exile based in Dharamshala, India. Tibetans traditionally believe him to be the reincarnation of his pre-decessors.

"By the end of the next decade almost half the world's population will live in countries that are water stressed, meaning they will not have enough water to meet the demands of their populations."

- Lester Brown

Lester R. Brown (born March 28, 1934) is an American environmentalist, founder of the Worldwatch Institute, and founder and president of the Earth Policy Institute, a nonprofit research organization based in Washington, D.C. BBC Radio commentator Peter Day calls him "one of the great pioneer environmentalists."

"In my garden, after a rainfall, you can faintly, yes, hear the breaking of new blooms."

- Truman Capote

Truman Garcia Capote (September 30, 1924 – August 25, 1984) was an American author many of whose short stories, novels, plays and nonfiction are recognized literary classics, including the novella Breakfast at Tiffany's (1958) and In Cold Blood (1965), which he labeled a "nonfiction novel." At least 20 films and television dramas have been produced from Capote novels, stories and screenplays.

Water in Love

"A woman would run through fire and water for such a kind heart."

- William Shakespeare

William Shakespeare (baptised 26 April 1564; died 23 April 1616) was an English poet and playwright, widely regarded as the greatest writer in the English language and the world's pre-eminent dramatist. He is often called England's national poet and the "Bard of Avon".

"What a woman says to her avid lover should be written in wind and running water."

- Catullus

Gaius Valerius Catullus (ca. 84 BC – ca. 54 BC) was a Roman poet. His surviving works are still read widely, and continue to influence poetry and other forms of art. Catullus came from a leading equestrian family of Verona, and according to St. Jerome he was born in the town. The family was prominent enough for his father to entertain Caesar, then governor of Gaul

"For true love is inexhaustible; the more you give, the more you have. And if you go to draw at the true fountainhead, the more water you draw, the more abundant is its flow."

- Antoine de Saint-Exupery

Antoine de Saint-Exupéry (29 June 1900—31 July 1944) was a French writer and aviator. He is best remembered for his novella The Little Prince (Le Petit Prince), and for his books about aviation adventures, including Night Flight and Wind, Sand and Stars.

"Absence in love is like water upon fire; a little quickens, but much extinguishes it."

- Hannah More

Hannah More (2 February 1745 – 7 September 1833) was an English religious writer and philanthropist. She can be said to have made three reputations in the course of her long life: as a poet and playwright in the circle of Johnson, Reynolds and Garrick, as a writer on moral and religious subjects, and as a practical philanthropist.

"A lifetime without love is of no account.
Love is the water of life. Drink it down
with heart and soul."

- Rumi

Mawlānā Jalāl ad-Dīn Muḥammad Balkhī, also known as Jalāl ad-Dīn Muḥammad Rūmī, but known to the English-speaking world simply as Rumi, (30 September 1207 – 17 December 1273), was a 13th-century Persian poet, Islamic jurist, theologian, and mystic.

"When you long with all your heart for someone to love you, a madness grows there that shakes all sense from the trees and the water and the earth. And nothing lives for you, except the long deep bitter want. And this is what everyone feels from birth to death."

- Denton Welch

Maurice Denton Welch (27 March 1915 - 30 December 1948) was an English writer and painter, admired for his vivid prose and precise descriptions.

"You see through love, and that deludes your sight, as what is straight seems crooked through the water."

- John Dryden

ohn Dryden (9 August 1631 – 12 May 1700) was an influential English ɔoet, literary critic, translator, and playwright who dominated the liter-ıry life of Restoration England to such a point that the period came to be known in literary circles as the Age of Dryden.

"Water is always a support or a healing thing apart from, you know, love or peace of mind."

- Nastassja Kinsk

Nastassja Kinski (born January 24, 1959) is a German-born American-based actress who has appeared in more than 60 films. In the late 1970s and throughout the 1980s, Kinski was widely regarded as an international sex symbol.

"Thousands have lived without love,
not one without water."

- W. H. Auden

Wystan Hugh Auden (21 February 1907 – 29 September 1973), who signed his works W. H. Auden, was an Anglo-American poet, born in England, later an American citizen, regarded by many as one of the greatest writers of the 20th century.

"O mind, love the Lord, as the lotus loves
the water. Tossed about by the waves,
it still blossoms with love."

- Sri Guru Granth Sahib

The Guru Granth Sahib or Adi Granth, is the holy scripture and the final
Guru of the Sikhs. It is a voluminous text of 1430 angs (pages), compiled
and composed during the period of Sikh Gurus, from 1469 to 1708.

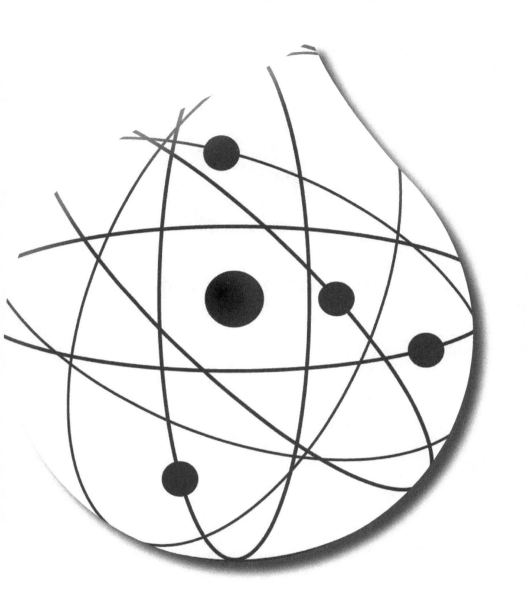

Water in Science

"Water is the driver of nature."

- Leonardo da Vinci

Leonardo di ser Piero da Vinci, (April 15, 1452 – May 2, 1519), was an Italian polymath: painter, sculptor, architect, musician, scientist, mathematician, engineer, inventor, anatomist, geologist, botanist and writer. Leonardo has often been described as the archetype of the Renaissance man.

"Water, the Hub of Life. Water is its mater and matrix, mother and medium. Water is the most extraordinary substance! Practically all its properties are anomalous, which enabled life to use it as building material for its machinery. Life is water dancing to the tune of solids."

- Albert Szent-Gyorgyi

Albert Szent-Györgyi de Nagyrápolt (September 16, 1893 – October 22, 1986) was a Hungarian physiologist who won the Nobel Prize in Physiology or Medicine in 1937. He is credited with discovering vitamin C and the components and reactions of the citric acid cycle. He was also active in the Hungarian Resistance during World War II and entered Hungarian politics after the war.

"All is born of water; all is sustained by water."

- Johann Wolfgang von Goethe

Johann Wolfgang von Goethe (28 August 1749 – 22 March 1832) was a German writer and statesman. His works include: four novels; epic and lyric poetry; prose and verse dramas; memoirs; an autobiography; literary and aesthetic criticism; and treatises on botany, anatomy, and color.

"All things that come into being and grow
are earth and water."

- Xenophanes

Xenophanes of Colophon (c. 570 – c. 475 BC) was a Greek philosopher, theologian, poet, and social and religious critic. Xenophanes is seen as one of the most important presocratic philosophers.

"Sustainability is not just about adopting the latest energy-efficient technologies or turning to renewable sources of power. Sustainability is the responsibility of every individual every day. It is about changing our behaviour and mindset to reduce power and water consumption, thereby helping to control emissions and pollution levels."

- Joe Kaeser

Joe Kaeser (born June 23, 1957) is the current CEO of Siemens AG, Berlin & Munich, a role he has been in since August 1, 2013. He sits on the boards of Allianz Deutschland AG, Daimler, and NXP Semiconductors. His honors include the Grand Cross of the Order of Entrepreneurial Merit and the 2017 Prize for Understanding and Tolerance, awarded by the Jewish Museum Berlin.

"Not all water is great for you. I drink a lot of water during the day, but I stay away from certain waters because their pH levels are low. Stick to alkaline waters with a higher pH. Trust me."

- Kawhi Leonard

Kawhi Anthony Leonard (born June 29, 1991) is an American professional basketball player for the Los Angeles Clippers of the National Basketball Association (NBA). He has also played for the San Antonio Spurs (2011-2018) and the Toronto Raptors (2018-2019).

"For me, being green means cleaning up the water. Water is the key. Start with water. You can't ignore the fact that nearly 80% of US waterways are potentially poisoned - benzene, solvents, heavy metals, pharmaceuticals."

- Erin Brockovich

Erin Brockovich (born June 22, 1960) is an American legal clerk, consumer advocate, and environmental activist, who, despite her lack of formal education in the law, was instrumental in building a case against the Pacific Gas and Electric Company (PG&E) of California in 1993 for contaminating drinking water. She is the president of Brockovich Research & Consulting.

"If you could tomorrow morning make water clean in the world, you would have done, in one fell swoop, the best thing you could have done for improving human health by improving environmental quality."

- William C. Clark

William C. Clark (born December 20, 1948) is the Harvey Brooks Professor of International Science, Public Policy and Human Development at the John F. Kennedy School of Government, Harvard University. Clark is a member of the USA's National Academy of Sciences and a Fellow of the American Association for the Advancement of Science. He received a MacArthur Fellowship in 1983.

"In every glass of water we drink, some of the water has already passed through fishes, trees, bacteria, worms in the soil, and many other organisms, including people...Living systems cleanse water and make it fit, among other things, for human consumption."

- Elliot A. Norse

Elliot A. Norse is a marine and forest conservation biologist. He has devoted his career to incorporating conservation biology into environmental decision making as a staff member or consultant for US federal agencies, international governmental organizations, scientific professional societies, conservation organizations, and foundations.

"An ocean traveller has even more vividly the impression that the ocean is made of waves than that it is made of water."

- Sir Arthur Stanley Eddington

Sir Arthur Stanley Eddington (December 28, 1882 – November, 22 1944) was an English astronomer, physicist, and mathematician. He was also a philosopher of science and a popularizer of science. The Eddington limit, the natural limit to the luminosity of stars, or the radiation generated by accretion onto a compact object, is named in his honor.

Water in Money

"The day, water, sun, moon, night - I do not have to purchase these things with money."

- Titus Maccius Plautus

Titus Maccius Plautus (c. 254–184 BC), commonly known as Plautus, was a Roman playwright of the Old Latin period. His comedies are among the earliest surviving intact works in Latin literature.

"The birds have no money in their pockets. They place their hopes on trees and water. He alone is the Giver. You alone, Lord, You alone."

- Sri Guru Granth Sahib

The Guru Granth Sahib or Adi Granth, is the holy scripture and the final Guru of the Sikhs. It is a voluminous text of 1430 angs (pages), compiled and composed during the period of Sikh Gurus, from 1469 to 1708.

"Money is like fire, an element as little troubled by moralizing as earth, air and water. Men can employ it as a tool or they can dance around it as if it were the incarnation of a god. Money votes socialist or monarchist, finds a profit in pornography or translations from the Bible, commissions Rembrandt and underwrites the technology of Auschwitz. It acquires its meaning from the uses to which it is put."

- Lewis H. Lapham

Lewis Lapham (born January 8, 1935) is an American writer. He was the editor of the American monthly Harper's Magazine from 1976 until 1981, and from 1983 until 2006. He also is the founder of a publication about history and literature entitled Lapham's Quarterly.

"But you I never understood, your spirit's secret
hides like gold sunk in a Spanish galleon,
ages ago in waters cold."

- Sara Teasdale

Sara Teasdale (August 8, 1884 – January 29, 1933), was an American lyrical
poet. She was born Sarah Trevor Teasdale in St. Louis, Missouri.

"We're still racing against the clock and we need to get more helicopters, more water, more tents and more money."

- Jan Egeland

Jan Egeland (born September 12, 1957 in Stavanger, Norway) was the United Nations Undersecretary-General for Humanitarian Affairs and Emergency Relief Coordinator from June 2003 to December 2006.

"Getting money is like digging with a needle, spending it is like water soaking into sand."

- Japanese Proverb

A Japanese proverb may take the form of: a short saying, an idiomatic phrase, or a four-character idiom. Although "proverb" and "saying" are practically synonymous, the same cannot be said about "idiomatic phrase" and "four-character idiom."

"Drink water, put the money in your pocket, and leave the dry-bellyache in the punchbowl."

- Benjamin Franklin

Benjamin Franklin (January 17, 1706 – April 17, 1790) was one of the Founding Fathers of the United States of America. A noted polymath, Franklin was a leading author and printer, satirist, political theorist, politician, scientist, inventor, civic activist, statesman, soldier, and diplomat.

"Wealth is like sea-water; the more we drink, the thirstier we become; and the same is true of fame."

- Arthur Schopenhauer

Arthur Schopenhauer (22 February 1788 – 21 September 1860) was a German philosopher known for his atheistic pessimism and philosophical clarity. At age 25, he published his doctoral dissertation, On the Fourfold Root of the Principle of Sufficient Reason, which examined the fundamental question of whether reason alone can unlock answers about the world.

"Water is best. But gold shines like fire blazing in the night, supreme of lordly wealth."

- Pindar

Pindar (Greek: Πίνδαρος, Pindaros; Latin: Pindarus) (ca. 522–443 BC), was an Ancient Greek lyric poet. Of the canonical nine lyric poets of ancient Greece, Pindar is the one whose work is best preserved.

"Accumulated wealth is saved by spending just as incoming fresh water is saved by letting out stagnant water."

- Chanakya

Chānakya (c. 350–283 BCE) was an adviser and prime minister to the firs Maurya Emperor Chandragupta (c. 340-293 BCE), and was the chief archi tect of his rise to power. Chanakya has been considered as the pioneer o the field of economics and political science.

Water in Wisdom

"Either you decide to stay in the shallow end of the pool or you go out in the ocean."

- Christopher Reeve

Christopher D'Olier Reeve (September 25, 1952 – October 10, 2004) was an American actor, film director, producer and screenwriter. He achieved stardom for his acting achievements, including his notable motion picture portrayal of the fictional character Superman.

On May 27, 1995, Reeve became a quadriplegic after being thrown from his horse in an eventing competition in Culpeper, Virginia. He lobbied on behalf of people with spinal cord injuries, and for human embryonic stem cell research afterward.

"I believe in getting into hot water - it helps keep you clean."

- G. K. Chesterton

Gilbert Keith Chesterton (29 May 1874 – 14 June 1936) was an English writer. His prolific and diverse output included philosophy, ontology, poetry, journalism, biography, Christian apologetics, fantasy and detective fiction.

"Some people are suffering from lack of work,
some from lack of water,
many more from lack of wisdom."

- Calvin Coolidge

John Calvin Coolidge, Jr. (July 4, 1872 – January 5, 1933) was the 30th President of the United States (1923–1929). A Republican lawyer from Vermont, Coolidge worked his way up the ladder of Massachusetts state politics, eventually becoming governor of that state.

"One can not reflect in streaming water.
Only those who know internal peace can
give it to others."

- Lao Tzu

Laozi was a philosopher of ancient China and is a central figure in Taoism
(also spelled "Daoism"). Laozi literally means "Old Master" and is generally considered an honorific. Laozi is revered as a deity in most religious
forms of Taoism. Taishang Laojun is a title for Laozi in the Taoist religion,
which refers to him as "One of the Three Pure Ones".

"A woman is like a tea bag, you can not tell how strong she is until you put her in hot water"

- Eleanor Roosevel

Anna Eleanor Roosevelt (October 11, 1884 – November 7, 1962) was an American political figure, diplomat and activist. She served as the First Lady of the United States from March 4, 1933, to April 12, 1945, during her husband President Franklin D. Roosevelt's four terms in office, making her the longest-serving First Lady of the United States. Eleanor Roosevelt also served as United States Delegate to the United Nations General Assembly from 1945 to 1952.

"Some people are making such thorough plans for rainy days that they aren't enjoying today's sunshine."

- William Feather

William A. Feather (August 25, 1889 - January 7, 1981) was an American publisher and author, based in Cleveland, Ohio. His large printing business, William Feather Printers produced catalogues, magazines, booklets, brochures and corporate annual reports.

"The one thing that a fish can never find is water; and the one thing that man can never find is God."

- Eric Butterworth

Eric Butterworth (Sept. 12, 1916 - April 17 2003) was among the leading spokespersons in modern times on "practical mysticism." Eric was considered a legend and spiritual icon in the Unity movement. The author of 16 best-selling books on metaphysical spirituality, a gifted theologian, philosopher, and lecturer, and for over 50 years a teacher of "practical Christianity."

"Be like water making its way through cracks. Do not be assertive, but adjust to the object, and you shall find a way round or through it. If nothing within you stays rigid, outward things will disclose themselves.

Empty your mind, be formless. Shapeless, like water. If you put water into a cup, it becomes the cup. You put water into a bottle and it becomes the bottle. You put it in a teapot it becomes the teapot. Now, water can flow or it can crash. Be water, my friend."

- Bruce Lee

Bruce Lee (November 1940 – 20 July 1973) was an actor, martial artist, philosopher, film director, film producer, screenwriter, and founder of the Jeet Kune Do concept. He is considered as one of the most influential martial artist of the 20th century, and a cultural icon.

"Being a fish out of water is tough, but that's how you evolve. I think that's scientifically accurate—I don't know, I had a liberal arts education."

- Kumail Nanjiani

Kumail Nanjiani (born 1978) is a Pakistani-American stand-up comedian, actor, podcast host and writer best known for writing and starring in the romantic comedy The Big Sick (2017) and for being a main cast member on HBO's comedy series Silicon Valley (2014–2019). In 2018, Time named him one of the 100 most influential people in the world.

"When time comes for us to again rejoin
the infinite stream of water flowing to and
from the great timeless ocean, our little
droplet of soulful water will once again flow
with the endless stream."

- William E. Marks

William E. Marks is an award-winning water author, poet, publisher, and Native American fluteartist, who was raised on an organic farm. His water research has been featured by various major news syndicates. He is the author of *The Holy Order of Water*.

Acknowledgments

It's true for me that there are many people that provide me the opportunity and support for writing and compiling this important book to the world.

First, I acknowledge my mom and dad, Judith Gabriel and Janos Gabriel for choosing to have children and providing me life so I can make this dream come true.

Second, I acknowledge my time in politics, that showed me the real need to focus on something larger than my limiting opinion and point of view.

Third, I acknowledge my children, Kyla Gabriel and Jeremiah Gabriel who provided me with the opportunity to live beyond my own needs and to think of the larger picture of life.

Fourth, I acknowledge Landmark Worldwide and all its transformational courses, especially the Landmark Forum - and the Communication Courses and the Team Management and Leadership Program - that reacquainted myself with my innerent abilities to make a global contribution and provided me with a profound joy of life.

Fifth, I acknowledge my friend and water mentor, William Marks, a true pioneer in the global water movement and whole book "The Holy Order of Water: Healing the Earth's Waters and Ourselves" opened me up to a new world of the power and magic of the blue stuff called H2O.

Sixth, I acknowledge WBCR-LP 97.7 FM in Great Barrington, MA for airing my radio show called "And So It Flows" and providing a home for international water media for the past 8 years.

Seventh, I acknowledge all the wonderful people in history who used water related language to express themselves.

Eighth, I acknowledge the incredible internet - including all the wonderful water quote websites and of course Wikipedia for providing great content and for inspiring me into action.

Ninth, I acknowledge my talented friend Heather Haines who provided me with the amazing book design.

Tenth, I acknowledge my publisher, IngramSpark for providing an avenue for publishing and distribution - allowing my dream to come to fruition.

Finally, I acknowledge all of my friends and family, along the way, who inspired me, held me to account and provided new points of view that challenged my comfort zone and provided me access to dream big, take action and accomplish more than I ever thought possible.

I thank you. I love you.

About the Author

Leslie Gabriel is an H2O activist, enthusiast and successful business owner of Watercheck.biz. Mr. Gabriel's devotion is promoting the benefits of water which he considers "the elixir of life."

After beating lifelong chronic skin rashes and other ailments, by simply using pure water to detox his body and mind, Leslie became a passionate believer in the power of water.

Mr. Gabriel's expertise is showcased as a successful radio show producer of 'And So It Flows,' the world's only show for H2O on WBCR-FM, in Great Barrington, MA.

Leslie is also an avid water blogger and founder of one of the first water blogs called WaterManBlog.com

Mr. Gabriel is also a video producer, director with a series of new media H2O relaxation videos called Zen Water Flix. He devotes a majority of this time on what he considers the most important movement of modern times...

The Water Sustainability Movement.

Leslie puts his money where his mouth is; as he and his company Water-Check.biz support water sustainability groups and projects in the US and around the globe. He is a public speaker about the pressing need of water sustainability and the need to transform our relationship to water and experience it in a different way - to a state of love and respect.

Leslie Gabriel is also a proud father of, who he calls, his "Big People" - Kyla Elianna Gabriel (25) and Jeremiah Noah Gabriel (21).

Leslie Gabriel is also an avid runner, hiker, skier, kayaker, camper, traveler and he loves to dance.

H2O Activists References

American Canoe Association - helps individuals and organizations under stand how paddlesport can contribute to the quality of life through en abling safe and positive paddling experience.
http://www.americancanoe.org

American Rivers - dedicated to protecting and restoring healthy, natu ral rivers and the variety of life they sustain for people, fish and wildlife
https://www.americanrivers.org/

Charity: Water - a nonprofit organization bringing lean and safe drinking water to people in developing nations. 100% of public donations directly fund water projects.
http://www.charitywather.org

Clean Water Action - using people powered democracy to work for clean affordable water, prevention of water pollution.
http://www.cleanwateraction.org

Clean Water Network - an alliance of more than 1,000 public interest or ganizations working together to strengthen and implement federal clean water and wetlands policy.
http://www.cleanwaternetwork.org

Cleanwater - conducts environmental education, advocacy programs and celebration to protect the Hudson River.
http://www.cleanwater.org

Coalition To Restore Coastal Louisiana - advocates for the restoration and preservation of the only great delta ecosystem in North America - the Mississippi River Delta.
https://www.crcl.org/

Coral Reef Alliance - a member supported, nonprofit organization dedicated to keeping coral reefs alive around the world.
http://www.coral.org

Cousteau Society - educating people to understand, to love and protect the water system of the planet, marine and freshwater, for the well-being of future generations.
https://www.cousteau.org/

Food And Water Watch - works with grassroots organizations and other allies around the world to stop the corporate control of our food and water.
http://www.foodandwaterwatch.org

Fluoride Action Network - dedicated to educate the public on the toxicity of fluoride compounds and the health impacts of current fluoride exposures.
http://www.fluoridealert.org

Frack Action - working to protect our water, air, and public health from the dangerous practice of hydraulic fracturing, or fracking.
http://frackaction.com

Global Water - an international non-profit, non-sectarian, non-governmental organization that is leading the worldwide effort to provide clean drinking water for developing countries.
http://globalwater.org

Global Water Partnership - supports countries in the sustainable management of their water resources.
http://www.gwp.org

Hydropower Reform Coalition - works to protect and restore rivers harmful hydropower dams.
http://www.hydroreform.org

Keepers Of The Waters - inspires and promotes projects that combine art, science and community involvement to restore, preserve and remediate water sources.
http://www.keepersofthewater.org

Lake George Association - advocates a reasoned approach to management of the Lake George watershed to ensure long-term stability of water quality and of the watershed's environmental and economic viability.
https://www.lakegeorgeassociation.org/

Marine Rivers - protects, restores and enhances the health and vitality of Marine's Rivers.
http://mainrivers.org

Marine Conservation Society, MCS - is the voice for everyone, in the United Kingdom and the world, who loves the sea. We work to secure a future for our living seas, and to save our threatened sea life before it is lost forever.
http://www.mcsuk.org

Ocean Futures Society - explores our global ocean, inspiring and educating people throughout the world to act responsibly for its protection.
http://www.oceanfutures.org

Oceana - campaigns to protect and restore the world's oceans.
http://na.oceana.org

Orca Network - dedicated to raising awareness about the whales, in particular the Orca of the Pacific Northwest, and the importance of providing them healthy and safe habitats.
http://www.orcanetwork.org

Pacific Rivers Council - one of the most influential rivers conservation groups in the country. Our mission is to protect and restore rivers, their watersheds and native aquatic species.
http://pacificrivers.org

Reef Relief - dedicated to preserve and protect living coral reef ecosystems through local, regional and global efforts.
https://www.reefrelief.org/

River Keeper - an advocacy group that monitors the Hudson River ecosystem and challenges polluters, using both legal and grassroots campaigns.
http://www.riverkeeper.org

Savannah Riverkeeper - protects the water quality of the Savannah River and the integrity of its watershed, and promotes an enlightened stewardship of this unique heritage.
http://www.savannahriverkeeper.org

Save Our Springs - protects the Edwards Aquifer of Texas, its springs and contributing streams, and the natural and cultural heritage of its Hill country watershed, with special emphasis on the Barton Springs Edwards Aquifer.
http://www.sosalliance.org

Sea Turtle Restoration Project - fights to protect endangered sea turtle populations in ways that meet the ecological needs of the sea turtles and the oceans and the needs of the local communities who share the beaches and waters with these gentle creatures.
http://seaturtles.org

Soil and Water Conservation Society - fosters the science and art of soil, water and related natural resource management to achieve sustainability.
http://www.swcs.org

South Fork Groundwater Task Force - an all-volunteer organization made up of concerned citizens from the Towns of Southampton and East Hampton Long Island, New York. Its goal is to protect the South Fork's groundwater from contamination, deple.
http://www.southforkgroundwatertaskforce.org

Tip Of The Mitt Watershed Council - here to protect the waters of Northern Michigan - some of the most important, diverse and pristine water resources on earth.
http://www.watershedcouncil.org

Water.org - nonprofit organization committed to providing safe drinking water and sanitation to people in developing countries.
http://water.org

Water Environment Federation - an international not-for-profit educational and technical organization of 40,000+ water quality experts.
http://www.wef.org

Water For People - helps the most impoverished people worldwide improve their quality of life by supporting sustainable drinking water, sanitation and hygiene projects.
http://waterforpeople.org

Wetlands Initiative - a nonprofit corporation dedicated to restoring the wetland resources of the Midwest to improve water quality, increase wildlife habitat and biodiversity, and reduce flooding damages.
http://www.wetlands-initiative.org

World Health Organization's WHO Website On Water, Sanitation and Health - dedicated to the reduction of water and waste-related diseases and the optimization of the health benefits of sustainable water and waste management.
http://www.who.int?water_sanitation_health/en/

World Water Council - an international water policy think tank that promotes awareness about critical water issues at all levels, including the highest decision-making level.
http://www.worldwatercouncil.org

World Water Rescue Foundation - a nonprofit foundation dedicated to protecting and preserving the world's water resources and ensuring the fundamental right of access to safe drinking water for all people.
http://www.wwrf.org/

WaterAid - an international Non-Governmental Organization (NGO) dedicated to the provision of safe domestic water, sanitation and hygiene to the world's poorest people.
http://www.wateraid.org

Photographic References

The following images were taken from Wikimedia Commons and are in the public domain:

- United States House of Representatives
- Martin Luther King, 1964
- John F. Kennedy, White House photo portrait
- Lyndon B. Johnson photo portrait
- Ralph Nader 1975
- Frederick Douglass (circa 1879)
- Portrait of Bertrand Barère de Vieuzac (1755-1841), French revolutionary politician and English spy
- Joseph Stalin
- Thomas Jefferson
- Enso (zen circle)
- Thales of Miletus
- Bodhisattva Gandhara Guimet
- Bhagavad Gita, a 19th century manuscript
- Lower Chinook chief from Warm Spring reservation, 1886
- John of Damascus
- Nathaniel Hawthorne
- Saint Francis Receiving the Stigmata by El Greco
- W. C. Fields, 1935
- Rodney Danagerfield, 1972
- Lewis Black Aviano
- Jacques-Yves Cousteau
- Photo of John Burrughs
- E. E. Cummings NYWTS
- Rachel Carson

- Henry David Thoreau
- Truman Capote NYWTS
- William Shakespeare
- Antoine de Saint-Exupéry
- Hannah More by Pickersgil
- Denton Welch - Self Portrait
- John Dryden Portrait
- Portrait of W. H. Auden
- Sri Guru Granth Sahib Nishan
- Self Portrait of Leonardo da Vinci
- Albert Szent-Gyorgyi
- Johann Wolfgang von Goethe, by Joseph Karl Stieler, 1828
- Xenophanes in Thomas Stanley History of Philosophy
- Arthur Stanley Eddington
- Bust of Plautus
- Filsinger, Sara Teasdale, portrait photograph. Date: July 11, 1919
- Courtesan, head-and-shoulders portrait, facing left, holding a scroll and chewing on the end of a brush
- Benjamin Franklin by Joseph Duplessis, 1778
- Arthur Schopenhauer by J Schäfer, 1859
- Chanakya artistic depiction, 1915
- G. K. Chesterton
- Portrait of Calvin Coolidge (1872-1933)
- Portrait of Lao Zi (Lao Tzu), Project Gutenberg
- Anna Eleanor Roosevelt Portrait
- Photo of Bruce Lee as Kato, from the TV series The Green Hornet
- The Kiss by Francesco Hayez
- Rutherford atom
- God Vishnu by Ramanarayanadatta astri
- The Thinker sculpture by Rodin

- Henrik Bentzon and Betty Nansen in "13 Øre" by Gladys B. Stern
- Hermann Hesse - Dutch National Archives, The Hague, Fotocollectie Algemeen Nederlands Persbureau (ANEFO), 1945-1989

The following images were taken from Wikimedia Commons and are attributed accordingly below. Images were converted to black and white. For more information on the licensure see: https://creativecommons.org/licenses/by-sa/2.0/deed.en

- Gorbachev & Reagan 1986 - Photo by: Official CTBTO Photostream
- Nelson Mandela - Photo by: South Africa The Good News
- Islamic Gallery British Museum - Photo by: LordHarris
- Joe Kaeser CEO of Siemens in Moscow 26 march 2014 - Photo by: President of the Russian Federation (www.kremlin.ru)
- Kawhi Leonard 2019 - Photo by: Chensiyuan
- Erin Brockovich - Photo by: Eva Rinaldi
- Steven Wright 1994 - Photo by: 48states
- Woody Allen, 2015 - Photo by: Adam Bielawski
- Jesus is coming.. Look Busy (George Carlin) - Photo by: Bonnie from Kendall Park, NJ
- Robin Williams Happy Feet premiere - Photo by: Eva Rinaldi
- Lily Tomlin Sept 2011- Photo by: Angela George
- Lewis H. Lapham - Photo by: kellywritershouse
- Russell Brand Arthur Premier - Photo by: Eva Rinaldi
- Tenzin Gyatso, 14th Dalai Lama in Trento in 2013 - Photo by: Niccolò Caranti
- Lester Brown - Photo by Agência Brasil
- Bust of Catullus, Italy - Photo by: Son of Groucho
- Nastassja Kinski - Photo by: 9EkieraM1
- Jan Egeland, on the panel discussion - Photo by: DFID - UK Department for International Development

- Bust of Pindar. Roman copy from original of the mid-5 century B.C. Napoli, Museo Archeologico Nazionale - Photo by: Stas Kozlovsky
- Christopher Reeve in Marriage of Figaro Opening night 1985 - Photo by: Jbfrankel
- Kumail Nanjiani - Photo by: Gage Skidmore
- William Feather III - Photo by William Feather III

Special photo attributions:

- William Clark - copyright of the image belongs to William Clark and is used with his express permission
- Elliot A. Norse
  https://www.seattleaquarium.org/blog/sound-conversations-elliott-norse-phd-march-7-seattle-aquarium
- Brad Stine - copyright of the image belongs to Brad Stine and is used with the express permission of the Brad Stine Team
- Eric Butterworth - copyright of the image belongs to Unity World Headquarters and is used with their express permission

The following photos were taken from pexels.com or unsplash.com, royalty-free photo websites that requires no author attribution.

- Mountain with water
- Man laughing
- Earth in hands
- Seljalandsfoss Waterfall, Iceland
- Money

CPSIA information can be obtained
at www.ICGtesting.com
Printed in the USA
BVHW030737050221
599006BV00078B/535